Go **BE A**
TRACKER

Thanks to the creative team:

Senior Editor: Alice Peebles

Designer: Lauren Woods and
collaborate agency

First published in Great Britain in 2015
by Hungry Tomato Ltd

PO Box 181

Edenbridge

Kent, TN8 9DP

A CIP catalogue record for this book is available
from the British Library.

ISBN 978-1-910684-15-3

Printed and bound in China

Discover more at
www.hungrytomato.com

Go Wild BE A TRACKER

By Chris Oxlade

Illustrated by Eva Sassin

HUNGRY TOMATO™

CONTENTS

TIME TO GO WILD

Where do you go to have fun? Have you tried exploring the great outdoors. No? Then it's time to go wild! Out in the wild you can track wild animals, explore ponds and rivers, and have a load of fun. So how about putting down your tablet, shutting down your laptop, switching off your games console, stepping out into the wild, and trying out some of the great activities in this book. Even if you live in the middle of a city, you can have a wild time in your garden or your local park.

In Go Wild – Be a Tracker, discover some of the skills needed to carefully follow tracks, hide secretly to watch animals, and catch and study all sorts of fascinating creepy crawlies.

WILD SAFETY

- Always ask an adult before going tracking in the wild. In particular, ask before going near or in water, or going to the coast.

- Ask an adult before you do any of the projects in this book.

- Beware of dangerous or poisonous wild animals.

- Always wash your hands after handling bugs or soil.

CARING FOR THE ENVIRONMENT

Always take care of the environment when you are in the wild. That means:

- Never damage rocks, animals or plants.

- Take special care to keep fires under control, and make sure a fire is out before you leave it.

FOLLOW THE TRACKS

ANIMAL TRACKING SKILLS

To watch animals in the wild, you first have to find them — and that means recognizing their tracks. Tracking skills will help you to follow animals by looking for footprints, paw prints and hoof prints, and other signs left by animals.

Red fox

Looking for tracks

A deer track in mud

1. The best places to search for animal tracks are muddy paths, the muddy banks of rivers, and beaches. Tracks will be clearer when the ground is damp, and early in the morning or in the evening, when the Sun is low in the sky. Walk slowly, looking carefully at the ground.

2. Try to match the tracks you find to the diagrams on this page. See if you can learn some common animal prints.

Rabbit

Cat

Grey squirrel

Deer

Dog

Black bear

It's a good idea to put a tape measure next to prints when you photograph them.

3. In winter, tracks are easy to see in fresh snow.

4. Try taking photographs of the tracks you find. Use the close-up setting on your camera, and photograph from low down and at an angle, to make them more visible. Take photographs of lines of prints as well as single prints.

5. If you find a trail of prints, see how far you can follow them – they might lead you to an animal's home.

Detective rat

Studying bird tracks

Sandy beaches and muddy riverbanks are good places to find bird tracks. Beware of sinking in soft mud on river banks though.

Chicken

Pigeon

Blackbird

Duck

Eagle

Crow

Sparrow

At the beach, look for tracks after the tide goes out; at the riverbank, look after the river level has fallen. Try to match any bird tracks you find to these diagrams

Making moulds

You can make copies of animal tracks in three dimensions. You'll need some plaster of Paris from a hobby shop.

1. Put a cardboard ring (such as the inside from a roll of sticky tape) around the print.

2. Mix a small amount of plaster of Paris, following the instructions on the packet. Carefully pour the plaster of Paris into the ring.

3. Allow the plaster of Paris to dry for about fifteen minutes, then carefully dig up the ring, taking a layer of soil with the plaster.

4. Take the ring home and leave it for a few hours to go hard. Then remove the ring and clean the dirt off the plaster.

5. Label your mould to show when and where you found the print, and what animal you think might have made the track.

Excuse me! Fox coming through!

More signs for tracking

Animals leave other clues besides their footprints.

As you are searching for tracks, keep an eye out for nibbled bits of food and pieces of fur.

A pine cone eaten by a squirrel

Tree bark stripped by a deer

A hazel nut opened by a mouse

Poo clues

You can also identify animals by the droppings (poo) they leave.

Look out for droppings on the ground, and try to match them to the references here. Don't touch the droppings!

Deer droppings

Fox droppings

Angry squirrel with poo on his foot!

Rabbit droppings

FOLLOW THE LEADER

MAKING AND FOLLOWING TRAILS

You can have fun laying trails in the wild for your friends to follow, and playing games where you creep up on your friends. These activities will be good practice for your tracking skills.

Laying a trail

1. Organize yourself and your companions into two teams — runners and trackers. The runners set off first, laying a trail as they go. Each time they reach a junction or change direction, they leave a sign to show which way they have gone. You can do this with sticks, stones, leaves or flour.

2. The trackers wait a couple of minutes and then try to follow the signs. Can they catch the runners?

EXAMPLES OF TRACKING SIGNS YOU CAN USE

Straight on

Gone Home

Not this way

Turn

Hunter and prey game

In this game, you (the hunter) try to creep up on a friend (the prey). Your friend has a water pistol, and will soak you if he or she hears you. The game will help you to practise moving quietly in the wild – and, if you are the one with the water pistol, to listen really carefully.

1. Choose a person to be the prey. He or she must stand in one place, with a filled water pistol, and wearing a blindfold. The hunters must move about 50 metres away. When everyone is ready, the hunters must try to creep silently up to the prey, and touch him or her before being heard.

2. If the prey hears a noise, he or she can fire the water pistol, aiming at where the noise came from, to try and soak the hunter.

Oops! These two have the game all wrong!

HIDE IN THE WILD

MAKING CAMOUFLAGE

When you are tracking small animals or watching birds, it's best not to let them spot you, otherwise they will get nervous and run or fly away. By wearing camouflage, you can easily blend in with the undergrowth. Or use camouflage to hide from your friends!

Camouflage face paint

2. Apply the paints to your face, in front of a mirror if possible. Use patches of colour to break up the shape of your face.

3. In an emergency, you can use mud or charcoal scraped from burnt sticks for face camouflage.

1. You can use face paints for this. Choose dark colours such as greens, browns and blacks, or make your own face paint by mixing skin lotion, cornflour and food colouring. Start with some lotion, mix the colouring in slowly, and then add cornflour to thicken it.

A camouflage shirt

2. Place some scraps of green cloth and brown cloth on a table. Lay your leaves on the cloth and draw around them with a marker pen. Draw about 30 leaf shapes altogether. Cut out the leaves.

1. Visit a wood or park and collect some large leaves. These can have just fallen to the ground, or be picked from trees.

3. Glue your cut-out leaves to a dark-brown or dark green T-shirt with fabric glue, overlapping them to cover most of the shirt.

A camouflage hat

1. Find a dark-coloured baseball cap or woolly hat. Collect up some twigs and small leafy branches, and attach these to the hat with sticky tape or safety pins.

Camouflage skunk!

SPOT THE FLYERS

BIRD AND BAT WATCHING

By building a bird hide and a bird box you can get close to birds in the wild, so you can study them and perhaps spot some you have never seen before.

Oh, if only I could find a home!

Making a bird hide

Set up this bird hide in woodland or on the shore of a lake, where there are plenty of birds.

2. Lean branches against the crossbar to make a screen. Leave a space in the centre of the screen to look through. Sit behind the screen and watch for birds, and use binoculars to view them more clearly.

1. Make two A-frames about 1 metre high by lashing together two pairs of sticks about 1.5 metres long. Lay a crossbar between them and tie the crossbar in place.

Terwit – terwoo!

Making a nesting box

A nesting box should attract small birds looking for a place to nest.

20cm 40cm 25cm 20cm 25cm

Front ● | Back | Side | Side | Base | Lid

15cm

25mm hole

20cm 25cm 12cm

I wonder who lives here...

1. Cut out shapes from a plank of wood, 15 centimetres wide and about 1.5 cm thick, as shown in the diagram.

2. Glue the parts together, but for the moment leave off the lid.

3. Glue a small block of wood inside the lid to stop it sliding off. Also put a small screw in each side of the box and the lid, and tie a string to the screws to keep the lid on.

4. Ask an adult to help you put up your box on a tree, at least two metres off the ground.

Looking for bats

Look for bats at dusk, when they emerge from their nests to hunt insects. Take an adult with you. Good areas to look are in woodlands and alongside rivers.

1. Stand still and look up towards the sky and listen. Look for small black shapes flying low and listen for high-pitched squeaks.

TWO COMMON BATS THAT YOU MIGHT SEE

Pipistrelle (UK)

Little brown bat (USA)

Hi guys!

15

DOWN BY THE WATER

EXPLORING PONDS AND RIVERS

You can find all sorts of creatures by exploring your local pond or stream. They live on the bottom of a pond or riverbed, in the water and on the surface. All you need is a simple net to find them.

Pond dipping

SAFETY NEAR WATER

Always take an adult with you when exploring near water. Be careful not to slip into the water on pond edges and riverbanks

1. Start by looking above the surface of a pond or river for dragonflies, mosquitoes and other flying insects. Then search the surface itself for bugs such as whirligig beetles and pond skaters.

2. Now dip a net into the water, move it slowly through the water and lift it out. Examine the net for creatures. Try dipping at different depths, and through the mud at the bottom of the water.

COMMON ANIMALS ABOVE AND ON THE WATER

Dragonfly

Pond skater

Whirligig beetle

Water boatman

16

3. Put your captured animals into a clean jam jar or a plastic pot with some pond water inside, and examine them with a magnifying glass. Release them before going home.

Pond snail

Fresh-water shrimp

Mayfly nymph

Sssso many pond animals to sssspot!

Stickleback

Newt

Looking after tadpoles

Try watching frogs' eggs grow into tadpoles.

2. When the tadploes begin to hatch, add a little fish food to the water.

3. After a few weeks, your tadpoles will start growing legs. This is the time to release them back to the pond.

1. Collect frogspawn in the spring by dipping a jar into a pond. Only take a small amount. At home put the frogspawn into a plastic tub with some water, and add a few stones in the bottom of the tub.

BUG BUSINESS

HUNTING AND CATCHING CREEPY CRAWLIES

The wild is full of bugs. Millions of them! They might not be as easy to see as larger animals and birds, but you can find them if you know where to look. Then you can catch and keep them.

Bug dinner

Put out tasty treats to attract some bugs to watch.

1. Make a sticky mixture of old mashed banana and sugar, smear a little on a stick and leave the stick outdoors, under a bush or stone. Return the next day to see what creatures have been attracted. You can also look at night with a torch.

2. If you want to study a bug more closely, carefully lock it into a container with air holes, where you can look at it with a magnifying glass.

COMMON BUGS THAT YOU MIGHT SEE

Did you see any of these common garden bugs?

Garden snail

Slug

Woodlouse

Ground beetle

Harvestman

I know I'm not a snail, but can I be your friend too?

Dead log safari

Rotting logs from dead trees are teeming with bugs! They feed on the rotting wood, and on other bugs and plants that live there.

BUG SAFETY

You may live in a place where there are biting or poisonous bugs and other animals. If you do, ask an adult to help you with this project, in case something potentially dangerous is lurking under the log.

1. First, find a rotting log (this will probably be in a wood). Examine the top and sides of the log, and pull off pieces of rotting wood to look underneath. Use a magnifying glass to study any bugs you find.

2. Lift away dead leaves and twigs to see under the log, but always put them back afterwards.

BUGS YOU MIGHT FIND IN A DEAD LOG

Black ant

Millipede

House spider

Snail friends

Beetle larva

Pitfall trap for bugs

Try setting up this simple trap to catch bugs that are exploring your garden during the night.

1. Take a large, clean jar to your bug-catching site (the woods or your garden). Dig a hole just big enough for the jar to fit into, so the neck of the jar is level with the ground.

2. Put a small piece of cheese in the jar to attract bugs. Place three small stones on the ground around the jar, and lay a flat rock, a piece of slate or an old tile on top. There should be a small gap between the cover and the rim of the jar.

3. Leave the trap to do its work overnight. What bugs did you catch?

BUGS YOU MIGHT FIND IN YOUR TRAP

Centipede

Beetle

Earwig

This trap is meant for bugs! Not for rodents!

A bug hotel

Here's how to build a luxury hotel –
well, luxury for bugs!

Can birds stay
here too?

1. Find an old wooden drawer or wooden box, about 50 x 30 centimetres.

2. Insert cardboard sheets cut to size and sleeves made of plastic bottles to divide the box into sections. Make short bamboo sticks, break up twigs, and gather stones and bundles of leaves.

3. Install all your materials in the box to complete the bug hotel.

4. Leave your bug hotel in the garden and check every day to see what's moved in...

It's holiday time for the bug family!

WATCH THOSE WORMS

MAKING A WORMERY

Soil is full of earthworms! You can catch some of these fascinating creatures and make a wormery (a special home) for them. Then you can watch them at work in the soil.

EARTHWORM FACTS

- Wriggling earthworms burrow through the soil and eat rotting leaves and vegetation.

- They help plants to grow by breaking up the soil and mixing air into it.

- There are around 6,000 different types of earthworm.

- Earthworms are male and female at the same time.

Build a wormery

Ask an adult to help you with this project.

30cm
30cm

1. You need two sheets of stiff clear plastic (acrylic or Perspex), about 30 centimetres square. Find an old wooden drawer or box, about 50 x 30 centimetres.

2. Next you need some strips of wood about 3 centimetres thick. Lay one of your sheets of plastic on a worktop. Then cut strips of wood to fit along three sides of the plastic, as shown. Glue the pieces on with waterproof glue.

5. Dig up some soil and carefully search through it for worms. Put the worms into a jar. Don't collect worms from a compost heap (they are not earthworms). Put a few worms into the wormery and watch them burrow down. Cover your wormery with an old cloth to keep out the light. After a few days you should be able to see the tunnels left by the worms as they burrow through the soil.

3. Glue the second plastic sheet on top of the strips of wood. Wait for the glue to dry completely.

4. Collect up some leaf mould, sand and soil. Put layers of mould, sand and soil into the wormery, one on top of the other. Add a little water to keep the layers damp.

6. Gradually the worms will mix up the layers of mould, soil and sand. If the top layer is beginning to dry out, add a little more water.

7. You can also make a simple wormery in a large plastic bottle.

Try not to eat the worms...

SNAIL SAFARI

KEEPING AND RACING SNAILS

Snails are easy to find in the wild. On this spread you can find out how to collect and keep them in a snail farm, and how to hold a snail race.

Safari bat!

Start a snail farm

Ask an adult to help you with this project.

1. FInd a container for your snails, such as an old, clear plastic box. Drill or puncture some holes in the lid to let in fresh air. Put plenty of food in the container for your snails: a mixture of leaves from different plants and chopped up old fruit works well.

2. Now find some snails from the wild or your garden. Search under leaves and rocks, and put the snails you find in a plastic box. At home, carefully put the snails into your snail farm. Leave the farm in a cool place out of direct sunlight to stop it from drying out.

3. Watch the snails over the next few days. Number some small stickers, then stick them carefully on the different snails to identify them.

4. Return all your snails to the wild after a few days.

Hold a snail race

Try holding a race with the snails from your farm!

Snails

10 centimentres

40 centimetres

What's this I hear about a safari?

1. Prepare a race arena by drawing two circles on a large piece of card, one about 10 centimetres across, and one about 40 centimetres across. Draw around pan lids or bowls to make the circles.

2. Mark your snails with stickers (see left) so you can identify the winner. Put all the snails in the centre ring and release them. The first snail to cross the outside line wins the race!

Snail (and a beaver) on safari!

SNAIL FACTS AND FIGURES

• Snails live on land, in lakes and rivers, and in the sea.

• The giant tiger land snail grows up to 30 cm long.

• Snail shells are made from calcium carbonate.

• A snail has thousands of microscopic teeth.

WINGS AND WEBS

CATCHING MOTHS AND SPIDER'S WEBS

Dozens of different types of moth flit about during the night, when you are asleep. You can catch them quite easily to study them. The mornings are a good time to look for spider's webs, which you can collect and keep.

Catching moths at night

Ask an adult to help you with this project.

1. Hang an old white sheet outdoors, so that it hangs vertically, like a wall. Set up a bright light, such as a camping lamp or bright torch, to light up the sheet. Wait until nighttime.

2. When it's dark, moths should be attracted to the light and land on the sheet. Examine them with a magnifying glass, and photograph them if you like.

Collecting spider's webs

1. First, find a spider's web. If a spider is in the middle of the web, blow gently and it should scuttle off. If it stays put, look for another web. Take a handful of talcum powder in your palm and blow across it, so that the talc blows onto the web.

2. Spray a sheet of black card with hair spray. Put the card behind the web and slowly move it forward until it touches the web.

3. Pull or cut away any threads at the edges of the card, and remove the card.

4. You can make your web picture permanent with artist's fixing spray.

SPIDER'S WEB FACTS

Spider's webs are incredible feats of engineering!

- The webs you are looking for in this project are called orb webs, and are made by orb-web spiders.
- Spiders' web silk is as strong as steel when stretched.
- Spiders use sticky and non-sticky threads to make their webs.

DON'T GET EATEN!

AVOIDING DANGEROUS ANIMALS

It's great fun to track and watch animals in the wild, but there are some animals you should never get too close to, because they could attack you if they're hungry or defending themselves. Some are dangerous because they are big, and some because they have poisonous bites.

Avoid insect bites

SNAKES AND SPIDERS

If you are tracking somewhere where there are poisonous snakes and spiders, make sure you don't accidentally step on one. When looking for bugs, turn over logs and stones with a stick, not with your hands. Also check your clothes and shoes for snakes and spiders before putting them on.

Bites from mosquitoes and other insects are unpleasant and can be dangerous. Steer clear of stagnant water, where mosquitoes live. Keep your skin covered, especially at night. Wear long trousers and long sleeves, and use a mosquito net (or cover up with a head scarf and glasses, above). Don't worry about looking silly!

A mosquito – one to avoid!

28

Beware of bears

100 yards

The black bear is the most common bear in North America.

1. Bears enjoy food! So when you are camping in bear country, put your food in bear-proof boxes, at least 50 metres from your tent, or in an airtight container hanging from a pole or thin branch in a tree. Never leave food in your tent! Do your cooking well away from your tent and keep your camp clear of smelly rubbish.

2. Make plenty of noise when you are moving around, so you don't surprise a bear. Stay away from dead animals, which could be their food. If you see a bear in the distance, don't go any closer, especially if it's with its young, or feeding.

3. If you are unfortunate enough to come face to face with a bear, stay calm and quiet, don't look it in the eye, and back away with you head lowered. Never turn and run, or climb a tree to escape – bears are better runners and climbers than humans!

DID YOU KNOW?

○ In some places in the world you can see amazing fossilized dinosaur tracks from millions of years ago. But you won't track down a dinosaur by following them!

○ The biggest dinosaur footprints found measure 1.5 metres across – that's three times as wide as an elephant's footprint. The dinosaur that made the prints must have been 25 metres long and weighed 40 tonnes.

○ In 1951 giant footprints were found in the snow of the Himalayas. They were not bear prints. Many people believe they were made by an ape-like creature that nobody has ever seen, known as a yeti.

○ Do you think you have a good sense of smell for tracking? You might have, but you're not as good as a bloodhound. They have a sense of smell a thousand times more sensitive than humans', and can sniff out the scent of people many days after they have left a place.

○ Many Aboriginal people in Australia are skilled trackers. An experienced Aboriginal tracker can tell the size, weight, age and gender of an animal from its tracks.

○ People often use the phrase 'snail's pace' to mean moving slowly. But what is a snail's pace? It's about 50 metres per hour.

These snails are moving at a snails' pace.

Hurry up! You two are so slow!

O If you catch a centipede, try counting its legs. Centipedes don't have a 100 legs as you might think. They normally have between 30 and 354 legs.

O The world's biggest bat is the Australian flying fox, which has a wingspan of more than 1 metre.

O A typical frog lays about 20,000 eggs in a pond. The eggs develop into tadpoles, but only one tadpole in 1,000 survives to grow into a frog.

O In healthy soil there will be about 250 earthworms per cubic metre.

O Some people think bears can't run downhill. They can – at about 60 kilometres per hour. That's twice as fast as you can run!

O The world's biggest moth is the colourful Atlas moth from south-east Asia. Its wingspan is 30 centimetres. Atlas moth caterpillars grow more than 10 centimetres long.

O Darwin's bark spider, which lives in Madagascar, weaves a web up to 25 metres across!

So many babies!

INDEX

THE AUTHOR
Chris Oxlade is an experienced author of educational books for children. He has written more than two hundred books on science, technology, sports and hobbies, including many activity and project books. He enjoys camping and adventurous outdoor sports including rock climbing, hill running, kayaking and sailing. He lives in England with his wife, children, and dogs.

THE ARTIST
Eva Sassin is a freelance illustrator born and bred in London. She has loved illustrating ever since she can remember, and she loves combining characters with unusual textures to give them more depth and keep them interesting.